THE BOOK OF HUMILITY

Alfonso Borello

Villaggio Publishing Ltd

CONTENTS

INTRODUCTION

Humility, often seen as a simple and unassuming virtue, holds the potential to transform individuals and societies in profound ways. It is a quality that can bridge divides, dissolve conflicts, and facilitate understanding. In today's world, where polarization and conflict abound, humility can serve as a powerful antidote.

This book delves into the concept of humility and its role in personal growth, relationships, and society. We explore how humility can help us overcome cultural and social barriers, navigate conflicts, and foster forgiveness. We also examine the challenges that can hinder the development of humility, such as ego and pride, fear and insecurity, and the lack of self-awareness.

Through the perspectives of psychologists, philosophers, educators, and political leaders, we gain a deeper understanding of the importance of empathy and cultivating a growth mindset. We also explore the impact of humility on our personal and professional lives, and how it can lead to greater success and fulfillment.

The book of humility is a call to action, inviting readers to embrace this essential virtue and integrate it into their daily lives. Whether you are seeking personal growth or hoping to make a positive impact on the world around you, the lessons and insights within these pages will guide you on a journey towards greater humility and a more fulfilling life.

SPECIAL NOTES FROM THE AUTHOR

Dear Reader,

I want to start by expressing my gratitude for choosing to read this book on the topic of humility. In a world that often values self-promotion and individualism, it can be difficult to recognize the importance of humility in our personal and professional lives. However, as you delve deeper into the pages of this book, I hope to share with you my insights on how practicing humility can lead to personal growth and development.

Throughout my own experiences and observations, I have come to understand the power of humility in building strong relationships, fostering empathy, and promoting growth mindsets. The concept of humility can be traced back to ancient philosophical traditions, and it is fascinating to see how it has evolved and remained relevant in modern times.

In this book, I explore the barriers that prevent us from cultivating humility, such as ego, pride, fear, and insecurity. I also provide practical strategies for developing self-awareness, practicing empathy, and fostering a growth mindset. I have included real-life examples, insights from experts in various fields, and thought-provoking questions to guide you on your own journey towards practicing humility.

I hope that by the end of this book, you will have a deeper understanding of the importance of humility and how it can positively impact your life. I encourage you to approach each chapter with an open mind and a willingness to reflect on your own experiences and attitudes towards humility.

Thank you for embarking on this journey with me.

Sincerely,
Alfonso Borello

Here some sources that gave me invaluable lesson in my research:

From "The Power of Now" by Eckhart Tolle: The importance of being present in the moment and letting go of ego-based thinking in order to cultivate a sense of humility and gratitude.

From "Daring Greatly" by Brené Brown: The connection between vulnerability and humility, and the courage required to be open and honest with oneself and others.

From "Mindset" by Carol Dweck: The concept of a growth mindset, which emphasizes the importance of embracing challenges and failures as opportunities for learning and growth.

From "The Art of Possibility" by Rosamund Stone Zander and Benjamin Zander: The transformative power of reframing one's perspective and embracing the mindset of possibility and abundance, which can lead to greater humility and openness.

From "The Alchemist" by Paulo Coelho: The idea that true fulfillment comes not from achieving external success or material wealth, but from cultivating a sense of purpose and following one's personal legend with humility and perseverance.

PREFACE

As I sit down to write this book on humility, I am reminded of the many times in my life when I have struggled with my own ego and pride. Whether it was in personal relationships, academic pursuits, or professional endeavors, I have come to realize that humility is not only a virtue but also a crucial skill that can help us navigate life's challenges with grace and wisdom.

Over the years, I have read countless books, listened to numerous lectures, and had many discussions about humility with friends, family, and colleagues. Through these experiences, I have come to appreciate the depth and complexity of this topic and the many ways in which it can be understood and applied.

This book is my attempt to distill some of the most important insights and lessons that I have learned about humility, drawing on a wide range of sources and perspectives. Whether you are a student, a professional, a parent, or simply someone who is interested in personal growth and development, I hope that this book will provide you with useful tools and ideas for cultivating humility in your own life.

Of course, I do not claim to have all the answers or to be a paragon of humility myself. Like all of us, I am a work in progress, and I continue to struggle with my own flaws and limitations. However, I believe that by exploring the many facets of humility, we can gain a deeper understanding of ourselves and the world around us, and ultimately, become better, more compassionate, and more effective human beings.

I invite you to join me on this journey of self-discovery and exploration, and to see where it takes us.

DEFINITION AND ORIGIN OF HUMILITY IN PHILOSOPHY

Humility is a virtue that has been celebrated by philosophers for centuries. Although its definition may vary depending on the philosophical tradition, humility is generally understood as a quality that involves recognizing one's limitations and being open to learning.

In ancient Greek philosophy, humility was celebrated as a form of wisdom. The philosopher Socrates, for example, famously proclaimed that he knew nothing, acknowledging his own limitations and inviting others to engage in a dialogue to discover the truth. This form of humility was seen as a way of seeking knowledge and understanding, rather than asserting one's own beliefs.

HUMILITY IN CHRISTIAN PHILOSOPHY

In Christian philosophy, humility was celebrated as a way of imitating the example of Jesus Christ, who humbled himself t serve others. The theologian Augustine of Hippo wrote that humility was the foundation of all virtues, as it allowed individuals to recognize their own sinfulness and seek forgiveness. This form of humility was seen as a way of cultivating a relationship with God and living a virtuous life.

Christian philosophy has a rich tradition of emphasizing the importance of humility as a virtue. The roots of this emphasis can be traced back to the Bible and the teachings of Jesus, and can also be found in the writings of Church Fathers.

HUMILITY IN EASTERN PHILOSOPHY

In Eastern philosophy, humility is often associated with the Taoist concept of wu-wei, which involves acting in harmony with the natural flow of things. Humility in this context involves recognizing one's place in the larger universe and avoiding arrogance or self-promotion. This form of humility is seen as a way of achieving inner peace and living in harmony with others and the natural world.

Humility In Taoism

In Taoism, humility is seen as a virtue that is closely linked with the concept of wu-wei, or non-action. The Taoist sage is humble and unassuming, allowing the natural course of things to unfold without trying to impose his or her will on the world. The Tao Te Ching, a key Taoist text, emphasizes the importance of humility in several passages.

Humility In Confucianism

In Confucianism, humility is seen as a key virtue that is

essential for living a moral and virtuous life. The Confucian sage is humble and modest, recognizing his or her own limitations and striving to improve himself or herself through learning and self-cultivation. Confucianism also emphasizes the importance of humility in relationships, as it encourages individuals to treat others with respect and humility.

Humility In Buddhism

In Buddhism, humility is seen as a key virtue that is essential for achieving enlightenment. The Buddhist practitioner must be humble and open to learning from others, recognizing his or her own limitations and striving to improve himself or herself through meditation and ethical conduct. Buddhism also teaches that humility is closely linked with compassion, as the humble person is able to empathize with the suffering of others.

Key Takes From A Session In Thailand With A Monk

In Buddhism, humility is seen as a crucial element of spiritual practice. The Buddha taught that humility is a key factor in developing wisdom and compassion, and that it is essential for cultivating a peaceful and contented mind.

According to Buddhist teachings, humility involves recognizing our own limitations and imperfections, and accepting them without judgment or criticism. This does not mean that we should have low self-esteem or diminish our sense of self-worth. Rather, it means that we should acknowledge our strengths and weaknesses with an open and non-judgmental mind.

One of the main ways in which humility is cultivated in Buddhism is through the practice of mindfulness meditation. By bringing a non-judgmental awareness to our thoughts, emotions, and physical sensations, we can begin to see how our own perceptions and biases color our experience of the world. Through this process of self-examination, we can begin to let go of our attachment to our own opinions and beliefs, and open ourselves up to new possibilities.

Another important aspect of humility in Buddhism is the practice of compassion. By recognizing our own flaws and limitations, we become more empathetic and understanding of others, and more willing to extend compassion and forgiveness to those who may have wronged us.

Stages Of Meditation

Concentration: In this stage, the focus is on developing the ability to concentrate the mind on a single point, such as the breath or a mantra. This helps to train the mind to stay in the present moment and not be distracted by other thoughts or external stimuli.

Mindfulness: In this stage, the focus is on developing awareness of one's thoughts, emotions, and physical sensations without judgment or attachment. This helps to develop a deeper understanding of oneself and one's experiences.

Insight: In this stage, the focus is on developing insights into the nature of reality, such as impermanence and interconnectedness. This helps to cultivate a sense of humility by recognizing that one is a small part of a much larger whole.

Loving-kindness: In this stage, the focus is on cultivating feelings of compassion and love for oneself and others. This helps to develop a sense of interconnectedness and empathy, which can lead to greater humility and understanding.

DEFINING HUMILITY IN CONTEMPORARY PHILOSOPHY

In contemporary philosophy, there are several definitions of humility that reflect its complex and multifaceted nature. One influential view of humility is that it involves a realistic assessment of one's own strengths and weaknesses, as well as a willingness to acknowledge and learn from one's mistakes.

According to this view, humility is not a matter of self-abnegation or a lack of confidence, but rather a recognition of one's own limitations and fallibility. This view of humility is often associated with the work of philosopher Bernard Williams, who argued that humility is a necessary corrective to the human tendency towards self-deception and overconfidence.

Another influential view of humility is that it involves a willingness to engage in self-reflection and self-criticism, in order to improve oneself and become a better person. This view of humility is often associated with the work of philosopher Martha Nussbaum, who argues that humility is essential for developing a sense of compassion and empathy towards others.

A third view of humility is that it involves a recognition of one's own interconnectedness with others and with the natural world. This view of humility is often associated with the work of environmental philosophers, who argue that humility is necessary for recognizing the limits of human power and for developing a more sustainable and responsible relationship with the environment.

Indeed, contemporary philosophy offers several different definitions of humility that reflect its complex and multifaceted nature. While these definitions may differ in some respects, they all emphasize the importance of humility as a virtue that is essential for personal growth, ethical conduct, and a healthy relationship with oneself and others.

IMPORTANCE OF HUMILITY

Humility is an essential virtue that has been highly valued in various philosophical traditions throughout history. Its importance can be seen in its many benefits for personal growth, ethical conduct, and social relationships.

Humility And Personal Growth

Humility helps individuals to recognize their limitations, weaknesses, and shortcomings. By acknowledging and accepting these aspects of oneself, individuals can develop a more realistic and grounded sense of self-awareness, which is essential for personal growth and self-improvement. Humility also enables individuals to learn from their mistakes and failures, as they are not hindered by pride or defensiveness.

Humility And Ethical Conduct

Humility is a key component of ethical conduct in many philosophical traditions. It promotes a sense of respect and empathy towards others, as individuals recognize that they are not inherently superior or inferior to others. This promotes a more egalitarian and compassionate approach to social interactions, which is essential for building healthy relationships and promoting social justice.

Humility And Social Relationships

Humility is also crucial for healthy social relationships, as it helps individuals to avoid conflicts and misunderstandings that can arise from arrogance, pride, or a sense of entitlement. It promotes a more collaborative and cooperative approach to social interactions, which fosters trust, respect, and mutual understanding.

Unquestionably, humility is a crucial virtue that has many benefits for personal growth, ethical conduct, and social relationships. Its importance can be seen in its many positive effects on individuals and society as a whole.

THE BENEFITS OF HUMILITY

Improved Relationships

Humility is a virtue that can have a profound impact on relationships, both personal and professional. When we practice humility, we are more likely to listen to others, acknowledge our own limitations, and show respect and empathy towards others. This leads to a more harmonious and empathetic relationship, where we are able to see things from different perspectives and work collaboratively towards common goals.

One of the key ways in which humility improves relationships is by promoting active listening. When practiced, we are more likely to listen to others without judgment or preconceived notions. We are also more likely to ask questions and seek clarification, rather than assuming that we already know what the other person is thinking or feeling. This promotes a more empathetic and compassionate relationship, where both parties feel heard and understood.

Increased Self-Awareness

Humility is a virtue that can lead to increased self-awareness, as individuals who practice humility are more likely to recognize their own limitations, strengths, and weaknesses. This self-awareness can help individuals to make more informed decisions, set realistic goals, and grow as individuals.

One of the key ways in which humility can increase self-awareness is by promoting introspection. When practiced, individuals are more likely to reflect on their own thoughts, emotions, and behaviors, rather than simply reacting to external stimuli. This introspection can help individuals to identify patterns and habits that may be holding them back, as well as strengths that they can build on.

Humility can also increase self-awareness by promoting a growth mindset. When individuals are humble, they acknowledge that they have room to learn and grow, rather than assuming that they already know everything they need to know. This mindset can help individuals to be more open to new experiences and ideas, and to view failures and setbacks as opportunities for growth, rather than as sources of shame or embarrassment.

Another way in which humility can increase self-awareness is by promoting mindfulness. When practiced, we are more likely to be present in the moment, rather than getting caught up in worries about the past or future. This mindfulness can help to better understand our thoughts, emotions, and physical sensations, and to respond to them in a more intentional and constructive way.

Enhanced Learning And Growth

Humility is a virtue that can have a profound impact on learning and personal growth. When we practice humility, we are more open to new experiences and ideas, and more willing to learn from others. This can lead to increased knowledge, personal growth, and professional development.

Personal And Professional Success

Indeed, this can lead to personal and professional success, as it promotes several key traits that are highly valued in both personal and professional settings. These traits include strong interpersonal skills, the ability to learn from mistakes, and the willingness to collaborate with others.

Collaboration

When we are modest, we recognize that we can benefit from the expertise and perspective of others. This can lead to improved problem-solving, increased creativity, and stronger teamwork.

COMMERCIAL BREAK FROM TIBET

L et's take a short break and see how the Dalai Lama would see humility.

"True humility is not thinking less of yourself; it is thinking of yourself less."

This quote highlights the Dalai Lama's perspective on humility as a way of thinking about oneself and others. According to the Dalai Lama, true humility is not about diminishing oneself, but rather, it's about shifting the focus away from oneself and toward others. It's about recognizing that one is part of a larger whole and that everyone has something to contribute.

The Dalai Lama also emphasizes the importance of humility in cultivating compassion and empathy. When individuals practice humility, they are more likely to be aware of the needs and experiences of others, which can lead to greater empathy and understanding. This, in turn, can lead to more meaningful connections with others and a greater sense of purpose in life.

Indeed, the Dalai Lama's perspective on humility emphasizes the importance of seeing oneself as part of a larger community, and of cultivating compassion and empathy for others.

THE RELATIONSHIP BETWEEN HUMILITY AND LEADERSHIP

Humility As A Key Leadership Trait

Humility is increasingly being recognized as a key trait for effective leadership in today's world. In this section, we will explore why humility is considered an important leadership trait, and what it entails.

One of the key reasons why humility is seen as an important trait for effective leadership is that it can help to build strong relationships with followers. Humble leaders are often more approachable, relatable, and empathetic, which can help to build trust and respect among their followers. This can lead to greater loyalty and commitment from followers, which is essential for achieving organizational goals.

Leaders are more likely to recognize the contributions and perspectives of others, and are more willing to work together to achieve common goals. This can lead to more creative and effective problem-solving, as well as a more positive and productive work environment.

Humility is also important for ethical leadership. Modest leaders are more likely to act in the best interests of their followers and the organization as a whole, rather than pursuing their own interests or agendas. This can help to create a culture of integrity and trust within the organization, which is essential for long-term success.

Humility As A Source Of Inspiration

Humility can also be a source of inspiration for leaders and their followers. When leaders demonstrate humility, they set an example for others to follow. This can inspire their followers to become more humble themselves, and to adopt a more collaborative and ethical approach to leadership.

Profound leaders can also inspire others by showing that success does not have to come at the expense of others. By acknowledging the contributions of their followers and working together to achieve common goals, they can create a sense of shared accomplishment and pride.

Furthermore, humble leaders can inspire others by showing that vulnerability is not a weakness, but rather a strength. By admitting their mistakes and limitations, they can demonstrate that everyone has room for improvement and that learning from failures is an essential part of growth.

Inspirational leaders often possess a strong sense of purpose and a clear vision for the future. By combining these qualities with humility, they can create a powerful leadership style that inspires others to work towards a common goal.

Indeed, humility can be a source of inspiration for leaders and their followers. Humble leaders can set an example for others to follow, inspire collaboration and ethical behavior, and show that vulnerability can be a strength. By combining humility with a strong sense of purpose and vision, leaders can create a powerful and inspirational leadership style.

Humility And Team Dynamics

Humility can also have a significant impact on team dynamics. When team members are led by a humble leader, they are more likely to feel valued and respected, which can lead to higher levels of engagement and motivation. Additionally, humility can foster an environment of open communication and collaboration, which can lead to more effective teamwork and problem-solving.

A humble leader is more likely to create an environment in which team members feel comfortable sharing their ideas and perspectives, without fear of being judged or criticized. This can lead to a more diverse range of ideas and perspectives, which can ultimately result in more creative and effective solutions.

Likewise, humility can help to prevent conflicts within teams. When team members feel that their opinions and contributions are valued, they are less likely to become defensive or confrontational. Instead, they are more likely to work together to find mutually acceptable solutions.

Also, humility can help to build trust within teams. When team members see that their leader is willing to admit their mistakes and shortcomings, they are more likely to trust that leader and be willing to take risks and try new things.

Indeed, humility can have a significant impact on team dynamics. Humble leaders can create an environment of open communication and collaboration, which can lead to more effective teamwork and problem-solving. Additionally, humility can help to prevent conflicts, build trust, and foster a sense of shared purpose and accomplishment.

THE ROLE OF HUMILITY IN CONFLICTS AND RESOLUTIONS

Humility As A Conflict Resolution Strategy

Humility can be a powerful conflict resolution strategy, both in personal and professional settings. When we approach a conflict with humility, we are more likely to listen to the other party's perspective, acknowledge our own faults and shortcomings, and be open to finding a solution that benefits both parties.

One of the main advantages of humility as a conflict resolution strategy is that it can help to de-escalate tensions and prevent conflicts from turning into power struggles. By acknowledging our own limitations and taking responsibility for our actions, we can demonstrate a willingness to work towards a resolution that benefits everyone involved.

Humility can also foster empathy and understanding between conflicting parties. When individuals approach a conflict with humility, they are more likely to see the other party as a fellow human being with their own aspirations, fears, and struggles. This can lead to a deeper sense of connection and a greater willingness to work together towards a mutually beneficial solution.

Humility In Negotiation And Mediation

Humility can play an important role in negotiation and mediation, which are key aspects of conflict resolution. Negotiation involves two or more parties who come together to reach a mutually acceptable agreement, while mediation involves a neutral third party who helps to facilitate the negotiation process.

In both negotiation and mediation, humility can be a valuable tool for building trust and creating a sense of collaboration. When individuals approach these processes with humility, they are more likely to listen to the other party's perspective, acknowledge their own limitations and biases, and be open to finding a solution that benefits everyone involved.

Humility can also help to create a more productive negotiation or mediation process by reducing the likelihood of defensive or hostile behaviors. When individuals are humble, they are less likely to feel threatened by opposing viewpoints or to react defensively. This can help to create a more open and productive atmosphere for negotiation and mediation.

Furthermore, humility can help to foster a sense of mutual respect between conflicting parties, which can be essential for building long-term relationships. When individuals demonstrate humility in negotiation and mediation, they show a willingness to work towards a mutually acceptable solution, rather than simply trying to "win" the negotiation or mediation process.

Without doubt, humility can be a powerful tool for negotiation and mediation, as it can help to build trust, create a collaborative atmosphere, reduce defensive or hostile behaviors, and foster mutual respect between conflicting parties. By approaching negotiation and mediation with a humble mindset, individuals can create an environment that is conducive to finding mutually beneficial solutions.

I beg the reader to consider what follows:

It is important to note that humility is not something that can be forced or faked. True humility comes from a genuine understanding and acceptance of one's limitations, strengths, and weaknesses. Acting with false humility or pretending to be humble can actually be harmful, as it can lead to a lack of authenticity and a disconnection from one's true self. It is important to cultivate humility through introspection, mindfulness, and a growth mindset, rather than trying to portray a certain image or persona to others. By embracing our true selves with honesty and humility, we can build deeper connections with others and lead more fulfilling lives.

Humility And Forgiveness And The Importance To Be Human

Humility can play a key role in the process of forgiveness. When we approach forgiveness from a place of humility, we are able to recognize our own limitations and acknowledge that we too have made mistakes in the past. This can help us to empathize with the person who has wronged us and to see them as fallible human beings rather than as villains or enemies.

Furthermore, humility can help us to let go of our own ego and the need to be right or to seek revenge. When we approach forgiveness from a place of humility, we are able to set aside our own pride and focus on the needs and feelings of the other person. This can lead to a more genuine and heartfelt reconciliation, rather than simply a superficial or forced apology.

Of course, forgiveness is a complex and multi-faceted process, and humility is just one of many factors that can influence it. However, by cultivating a spirit of humility, we can open ourselves up to a deeper understanding of ourselves and others, and create the space for true forgiveness and healing to take place.

WHAT IF YOU FAILED WITH DIGNITY AND HUMILITY

If you have failed with dignity and humility, it is important to take responsibility for your actions and apologize from the heart. Here are some steps you can follow:

Acknowledge the mistake: Start by acknowledging what you did wrong and take responsibility for your actions. Be sincere in your apology and avoid making excuses or justifying your behavior.

Express remorse: Show that you understand the impact of your actions and express genuine remorse for any harm caused. This will help the other person see that you are truly sorry and willing to make things right.

Make amends: Offer to make things right in whatever way you can. This might involve apologizing in person, making restitution, or taking steps to prevent the same mistake from happening again in the future.

Listen: Allow the other person to express their feelings and concerns. Be open to their feedback and take the time to listen to their perspective. This will show that you value their feelings and are committed to making things right.

Follow through: Finally, make sure to follow through on any promises you make. If you say you will make amends, do so in a timely and effective manner. This will help rebuild trust and show that you are committed to making things right.

Remember that delivering a sincere apology from the heart takes courage and humility. By taking responsibility for your actions, expressing remorse, making amends, listening to feedback, and following through on your promises, you can show that you are truly sorry and committed to doing better in the future.

Example Of A Business Apology

Dear valued customers,

We would like to sincerely apologize for the recent issue with our product. We understand that it has caused inconvenience and frustration for many of you, and we want to take responsibility for our mistake.

We have identified the root cause of the problem and are taking immediate steps to address it. We are also implementing new measures to ensure that this type of issue does not happen again in the future.

We value your trust and loyalty and are committed to making things right. If you have been impacted by this issue, please contact our customer service team for assistance.

Thank you for your understanding and patience.

Sincerely,

[Company Name]

From The Heart, Minimalistic

I'm sorry, but I need to tell you that I feel an immense sense of guilt and regret. My actions were completely unacceptable and I take full responsibility for the hurt that I have caused you. I know that my behavior was wrong and I can't begin to express how sorry I am. I understand that apologies can't undo the damage that has been done, but I hope that in some small way, it can begin to repair the trust and respect that we once shared. I want you to know that I'm committed to doing whatever it takes to make things right and to prove to you that I'm worthy of your forgiveness. I promise to learn from this experience and to become a better person, not just for you, but for myself as well. Please know that I deeply regret my actions and I will work tirelessly to make things right.

OBSTACLES TO CULTIVATING HUMILITY

Cultural And Social Barriers

One of the reasons why humility may be difficult to understand or practice in certain cultures or social contexts is due to the presence of cultural and social barriers.

For example, in individualistic societies such as the United States, there is often an emphasis on self-promotion and individual achievement. This can lead to a culture where humility is seen as weakness, and where people are encouraged to assert their dominance and showcase their accomplishments.

In addition, certain social and professional contexts may also make it difficult to practice humility. In highly competitive environments such as sports or business, for example, there may be a strong emphasis on winning and beating the competition, which can make it difficult to value humility or collaboration.

However, it is important to recognize that cultural and social barriers are not insurmountable, and that it is possible to cultivate a more humble and empathetic approach to life and leadership. By recognizing the importance of humility, and actively working to develop this trait in ourselves and others, we can create a more compassionate, collaborative, and equitable society.

Ego And Pride

Another barrier to practicing humility is the presence of ego and pride. Ego refers to a person's sense of self-importance or self-esteem, while pride refers to an excessive or inflated sense of one's own accomplishments or abilities.

Both ego and pride can make it difficult for a person to practice humility, as they may cause a person to focus primarily on their own interests and accomplishments, rather than valuing the perspectives and achievements of others.

In addition, the presence of ego and pride can also make it difficult for a person to acknowledge their own limitations and weaknesses, which is a key component of humility.

In psychology, ego and pride are often viewed as important components of a person's personality and self-concept.

Ego is typically seen as an important aspect of healthy personality development, as it allows a person to develop a sense of self-esteem, self-worth, and confidence in their abilities. However, when ego becomes overly inflated or rigid, it can lead to negative outcomes such as arrogance, narcissism, and a lack of empathy for others.

Pride is also viewed as a complex aspect of personality, with some psychologists viewing it as a positive emotion that promotes self-esteem and confidence, while others see it as a negative emotion that can lead to harmful behaviors such as aggression and dominance.

Overall, the role of ego and pride in human psychology is complex and multifaceted. While both are important components of healthy personality development, it is important to maintain a balance between a healthy sense of self-esteem and an excessive or rigid ego or pride, which can lead to negative outcomes for both the individual and those around them.

The negative aspects of pride and ego can be addressed and managed through various psychological interventions and personal practices.

One approach that is often used is cognitive-behavioral therapy (CBT), which focuses on identifying and changing negative thought patterns and behaviors that contribute to excessive pride and ego. Through CBT, individuals can learn to challenge distorted beliefs and perceptions about themselves and others, and develop healthier ways of thinking and relating to others.

Other approaches that may be effective in addressing excessive pride and ego include mindfulness meditation, which can help individuals develop greater self-awareness and reduce their attachment to ego-driven thoughts and emotions, and psychoanalytic therapy, which can help individuals explore and address underlying psychological conflicts and motivations that may contribute to excessive pride and ego.

Ultimately, overcoming excessive pride and ego requires a willingness to acknowledge one's own limitations and vulnerabilities, and a commitment to ongoing personal growth and development. While it may be challenging, with the right support and interventions, it is possible to cultivate a more humble and empathetic approach to life and relationships.

To overcome these barriers, it is important to recognize the negative impact that ego and pride can have on our relationships and our ability to lead effectively. By focusing on the needs and interests of others, and by acknowledging our own limitations and fallibility, we can begin to cultivate a more humble and empathetic approach to life and leadership.

Fear And Insecurity

Fear and insecurity can also play a role in preventing people from practicing humility in conflicts and resolutions.

In many cases, individuals may feel threatened or vulnerable in situations of conflict, and may respond with defensiveness, aggression, or other defensive strategies that are rooted in a fear of being harmed or attacked. This can make it difficult for them to engage in constructive dialogue and problem-solving, and can lead to further escalation of the conflict.

Insecurity can also play a role in preventing people from practicing humility, as individuals may feel the need to assert themselves or prove their worth in order to compensate for feelings of inadequacy or low self-esteem. This can lead to a focus on winning or being right, rather than on finding mutually acceptable solutions and building positive relationships with others.

To overcome these barriers, it is important for individuals to develop greater self-awareness and emotional intelligence, and to learn to recognize and manage their own fears and insecurities. This can involve cultivating mindfulness and self-compassion, developing effective communication skills, and seeking out support and guidance from trusted mentors, peers, or mental health professionals. By addressing these underlying psychological factors, individuals can become more open, receptive, and humble in their approach to conflicts and resolutions, and can build stronger and more positive relationships with others.

STRATEGIES FOR DEVELOPING HUMILITY

Cultivating Self-Awareness

Cultivating self-awareness is an essential step towards developing humility. By understanding our own strengths and weaknesses, biases, and limiting beliefs, we can better understand and appreciate the perspectives and experiences of others.

One way to cultivate self-awareness is through introspection and reflection. This might involve taking time each day to reflect on our thoughts, emotions, and behaviors, and to ask ourselves questions about our motivations and reactions to different situations. Journaling, meditation, and mindfulness practices can also be useful tools for developing self-awareness.

Another important aspect of cultivating self-awareness is seeking feedback from others. This may involve actively soliciting constructive criticism and feedback from friends, family, colleagues, or mentors, and being open to receiving and integrating their insights and perspectives.

By developing greater self-awareness, we can become more open-minded, empathetic, and compassionate, and can better recognize the contributions and value of others in our lives. This can in turn help us to become more humble and effective leaders, collaborators, and human beings.

From a psychological perspective, self-awareness refers to an individual's ability to accurately perceive and understand their own emotions, thoughts, and behaviors, and to recognize the ways in which these internal experiences are influenced by external factors and social contexts.

According to research in psychology, cultivating self-awareness can have a wide range of benefits for mental health and well-being. For example, individuals with higher levels of self-awareness tend to experience less stress, have better coping skills, and are more resilient in the face of adversity. They also tend to have more satisfying relationships, and may be more successful in their personal and professional lives.

Psychologists may use a variety of techniques to help individuals develop greater self-awareness, including cognitive-behavioral therapy, mindfulness-based interventions, and emotion-focused therapy. These techniques may involve helping clients identify and challenge negative thoughts and beliefs, cultivate greater awareness of their emotions and behaviors, or develop more effective coping strategies.

From a creative perspective, self-awareness can also be a valuable tool for personal growth and artistic expression. Being self-aware allows individuals to better understand their own strengths and weaknesses, and to use this knowledge to refine their creative process and produce more authentic and meaningful work.

For example, a writer who is self-aware may be better able to identify their own unique voice and style, and to use this to create more compelling and resonant stories. Similarly, a musician who is self-aware may be better able to tap into their own emotions and experiences, and to use this to create music that is more authentic and relatable.

In addition to enhancing artistic expression, self-awareness can also be a powerful tool for personal growth and self-discovery. By becoming more aware of our own thoughts, feelings, and behaviors, we can gain a deeper understanding of ourselves and our place in the world. This can lead to greater self-acceptance, greater empathy and compassion for others, and a greater sense of purpose and meaning in life.

Self-awareness has been explored and explained by many great thinkers throughout history, each offering their own unique perspective. Here are a few examples:

Socrates: "The unexamined life is not worth living." Socrates believed that self-awareness was essential for a fulfilling life. He argued that individuals should constantly examine their own beliefs and actions to better understand themselves and their place in the world.

Carl Jung: "Your vision will become clear only when you can look into your own heart. Who looks outside, dreams; who looks inside, awakes." Jung believed that self-awareness was essential for personal growth and spiritual development. He saw self-awareness as a process of exploring the unconscious mind and integrating it with the conscious mind.

Daniel Goleman: "Self-awareness is the foundation of emotional intelligence." Goleman popularized the concept of emotional intelligence and argued that self-awareness was a key component of it. He defined self-awareness as the ability to recognize and understand one's own emotions and their impact on others.

Eckhart Tolle: "To be aware of a single shortcoming within oneself is more useful than to be aware of a thousand in somebody else." Tolle emphasized the importance of self-awareness in developing a deeper sense of inner peace and enlightenment. He believed that self-awareness involved being fully present in the present moment and observing one's thoughts and emotions without judgment.

Without doubt, these thinkers and many others have emphasized the importance of self-awareness for personal growth, emotional intelligence, and spiritual development.

Practicing Empathy

Practicing empathy is an important aspect of cultivating humility. Empathy is the ability to understand and share the feelings of another person. It involves putting oneself in another person's shoes and seeing the world from their perspective.

One way to practice empathy is to actively listen to others without judgment. This means giving them your full attention, asking questions to clarify their perspective, and reflecting back what you have heard to ensure that you have understood them correctly.

Another way to practice empathy is to engage in perspective-taking exercises. This involves intentionally imagining what it might be like to be in someone else's position, particularly if that person is from a different cultural, socioeconomic, or demographic background than yourself. By doing this, you can gain a deeper understanding of their experiences and challenges, which can help you to be more compassionate and understanding towards them.

From a scientific perspective, empathy is a complex process that involves multiple brain regions and neural networks. Studies have shown that when we experience empathy, our brains activate mirror neurons, which allow us to feel and understand the emotions of others. This can lead to an increase in prosocial behavior, as we are more likely to help others when we can empathize with them.

Empathy is also linked to a range of positive outcomes, such as increased well-being, better mental health, and stronger social connections. By practicing empathy, we can improve our ability to connect with others, understand their needs and perspectives, and build stronger relationships. This can be particularly important in healthcare settings, where empathy can help healthcare providers better understand their patients' needs and provide more effective care.

Fostering A Growth Mindset

Fostering a growth mindset is an essential aspect of cultivating humility. Having a growth mindset means believing that one's abilities and intelligence can be developed through dedication and hard work, rather than being fixed traits that cannot be changed.

A growth mindset enables individuals to view challenges and failures as opportunities for growth, rather than setbacks. It allows individuals to embrace the learning process and persevere through difficult times. This type of mindset fosters a sense of humility by acknowledging that there is always more to learn and that no one has all the answers.

There are many ways to foster a growth mindset, including:

Emphasizing effort over innate ability: Praising effort and hard work rather than innate abilities can help individuals adopt a growth mindset.

Encouraging risk-taking and exploration: Encouraging individuals to take risks and explore new ideas and perspectives can help them develop a growth mindset.

Embracing failure as an opportunity for growth: Instead of viewing failure as a setback, encouraging individuals to embrace it as an opportunity to learn and grow can help foster a growth mindset.

Promoting a love of learning: Encouraging a love of learning and a curiosity about the world can help individuals adopt a growth mindset by recognizing that there is always more to discover and understand.

By fostering a growth mindset, individuals can develop a sense of humility by recognizing that there is always more to learn and that failure is simply an opportunity for growth.

HOW HUMILITY IS BECOMING A KEY COMPONENT IN EDUCATION

Humility is not always emphasized in traditional education systems, which tend to prioritize competition, individual achievement, and standardized testing. However, some educators and schools are recognizing the importance of teaching humility and are incorporating it into their curriculum.

For example, some schools are using programs that focus on social and emotional learning (SEL), which includes developing skills such as empathy, self-awareness, and responsible decision-making. These programs can help students to develop a better understanding of themselves and others, and to learn how to work effectively in groups.

Additionally, some universities and colleges have begun to integrate humility into their leadership and professional development programs, recognizing that humility is a key trait of effective leaders and a necessary component for success in many fields.

It must be noted that while humility may not always be explicitly taught in traditional education systems, there are efforts underway to incorporate it into education at all levels.

CONCLUSION

Uncovering The Hidden Forces That Drive Our Egos And How Humility Can Help Us Achieve True Self-Awareness.

If I would approach the topic of humility from a psychoanalytic perspective. Humility, or the lack thereof, can be seen as a manifestation of one's ego, which is the conscious part of the psyche that regulates our behavior and sense of identity.

According to psychoanalytic theory, the ego develops as a result of the interactions between the individual and their environment. Individuals who have experienced significant trauma or lack proper nurturing during their early years may develop a weaker sense of ego, which can manifest as feelings of insecurity, low self-esteem, and a lack of confidence.

On the other hand, those with a strong sense of ego may develop a more inflated sense of self, leading to arrogance and a lack of humility. From this perspective, humility can be seen as a healthy balance between the two extremes of a weak and inflated ego.

Furthermore, humility can also be viewed as a manifestation of the defense mechanism of repression, which is the unconscious act of pushing unwanted or uncomfortable thoughts and feelings out of awareness. By acknowledging and accepting our limitations, weaknesses, and mistakes, we can prevent these aspects of ourselves from being repressed and causing further psychological distress.

Briefly, humility can be viewed through a psychoanalytic lens as a healthy balance between a weak and inflated sense of ego and as a defense mechanism that allows for the acceptance of one's limitations and imperfections.

In Real Life

Humility is an important concept in real life because it helps individuals to acknowledge their limitations, accept criticism, and learn from their mistakes. By recognizing their fallibility, individuals become more open to learning and growth, and are better equipped to handle challenges and setbacks. Humility also promotes a sense of empathy and understanding towards others, which can lead to stronger relationships and more effective communication. In addition, humility can be a key component of leadership, as it allows leaders to prioritize the needs of their team and work towards common goals. Overall, humility is a valuable trait that can help individuals navigate both personal and professional challenges, and cultivate meaningful connections with others.

Another reason behind the concept of humility in real life is the recognition that success is often the result of collective effort rather than individual talent or merit. While individual contributions and achievements should be acknowledged, humility reminds us that we are not entirely self-made and that we owe a debt of gratitude to those who have helped us along the way. This can range from mentors who have guided us, to colleagues who have supported us, to family and friends who have provided emotional and practical support. By recognizing and expressing gratitude for these contributions, we can cultivate a sense of humility and a deeper appreciation for the importance of relationships and community.

Humility can also help us navigate the complexities of modern life and work, which often require collaboration and compromise. In a world where there are often competing interests and conflicting viewpoints, humility allows us to approach others with an open mind and a willingness to listen and learn. This can lead to more productive and fulfilling relationships, both personally and professionally, as we seek to understand others' perspectives and work towards common goals.

Without doubt, the concept of humility in real life is rooted in a recognition of our own limitations and fallibility, as well as the importance of relationships and community. By cultivating humility, we can become more self-aware, empathetic, and collaborative, and ultimately lead more fulfilling and meaningful lives.

It Would Be Unfair Not To Mention Some Historical Figures Who Have Been Known For Their Humility

Mahatma Gandhi: He was known for his humility and simplicity, and often lived a simple life in order to set an example for others. He believed in serving others and putting their needs before his own.

Mother Teresa: She devoted her life to serving the poor and sick, and was known for her humility and compassion. Despite her fame and recognition, she always remained humble and focused on her mission of serving others.

Nelson Mandela: He was a champion of human rights and social justice, and often demonstrated humility by listening to others and acknowledging his own mistakes. He believed in the power of forgiveness and reconciliation, and demonstrated these qualities during his leadership of South Africa.

Martin Luther King Jr.: He was a leader of the civil rights movement in the United States, and demonstrated humility by putting the needs of the community before his own personal interests. He often spoke about the importance of serving others and working towards the greater good.

Albert Schweitzer: He was a physician and philosopher who

dedicated his life to serving others, particularly in Africa. He believed in the power of humility and service, and demonstrated these qualities throughout his life.

These historical figures demonstrate that humility is an important quality for leaders and individuals who seek to make a positive impact on the world.

Final Thoughts

I believe that humility is a vital trait that can help us improve in many aspects of our lives. By recognizing our limitations and weaknesses, we can become more self-aware and open-minded, which in turn can lead to personal growth and development.

Practicing empathy and fostering a growth mindset are two ways to cultivate humility. By putting ourselves in someone else's shoes, we can gain a better understanding of their perspective and develop a more compassionate outlook. By embracing challenges and failures as opportunities for growth, we can develop resilience and a willingness to learn.

However, it's important to acknowledge that practicing humility is not always easy. We live in a culture that often values individualism and self-promotion over modesty and humility. Overcoming our own egos and fears can be a challenging process, but by embracing humility as a core value, we can work towards becoming more grounded, compassionate, and successful individuals.

With confidence, I believe that humility is a crucial trait that can help us become better people, leaders, and global citizens. By striving to cultivate humility in our daily lives, we can make a positive impact on the world around us and become the best versions of ourselves.

DRIVEN BY INSPIRATION IN THE EXPLANATION, HERE ARE SOME DICTIONARY DEFINITIONS OF HUMILITY

Oxford Languages: "The quality of having a modest or low view of one's importance."

Merriam-Webster: "Freedom from pride or arrogance: the quality or state of being humble."

Cambridge Dictionary: "The quality of not being proud because you are aware of your bad qualities."

Collins English Dictionary: "Humility is the quality of being humble and means that you have a low opinion of your own importance."

Dictionary.com: "The quality or condition of being humble;

modest opinion or estimate of one's own importance, rank, etc."

QUIZ

1. What are the three key traits that can help cultivate humility?

a) Self-awareness, empathy, and a fixed mindset
b) Self-awareness, sympathy, and a growth mindset
c) Self-awareness, empathy, and a growth mindset
d) Self-esteem, sympathy, and a growth mindset

2. Who are some historical figures that embody humility?

a) Winston Churchill and Abraham Lincoln
b) Mother Teresa and Nelson Mandela
c) Bill Gates and Steve Jobs
d) Albert Einstein and Isaac Newton

3. What are some benefits of humility?

a) Increased arrogance and the ability to dominate others
b) Increased resilience and the ability to learn from failure
c) Decreased empathy and understanding of others
d) Decreased self-awareness and personal growth

4. What is the role of education in fostering humility?

a) Education places a high emphasis on the importance of humility
b) Education largely ignores the importance of humility
c) Education fosters humility through the development of

critical thinking skills

    d) Education fosters humility through the promotion of individual achievement

5. What are some potential chapters in a book on humility?

a) The Benefits of Arrogance
b) How to Dominate Others: A Guide to Narcissism
c) Cultivating Humility Through Self-Awareness and Empathy
d) Why Self-Esteem is the Key to Success.

Answers on next page.

Answers:

1. c) Self-awareness, empathy, and a growth mindset
2. b) Mother Teresa and Nelson Mandela
3. b) Increased resilience and the ability to learn from failure
4. b) Education largely ignores the importance of humility
5. c) Cultivating Humility Through Self-Awareness and Empathy

BOOKS TO READ

Here are some books you may want to read related to the topics covered in "The Book of Humility":

"Man's Search for Meaning" by Viktor E. Frankl - This book explores the meaning of life and the importance of finding purpose in difficult circumstances.

"The Power of Now" by Eckhart Tolle - This book discusses the importance of living in the present moment and how it can lead to greater happiness and fulfillment.

"Daring Greatly" by Brené Brown - This book explores the role of vulnerability in building strong relationships and developing a sense of self-worth.

"Meditations" by Marcus Aurelius - This book is a collection of writings by the Roman emperor and philosopher, exploring the nature of existence, human behavior, and the importance of humility.

"The 7 Habits of Highly Effective People" by Stephen R. Covey - This book provides practical advice for achieving personal and professional success, including tips on developing a growth mindset and building strong relationships.

"The Tao Te Ching" by Lao Tzu - This book is a classic text of Taoist philosophy, exploring the importance of humility, simplicity, and living in harmony with the natural world.

"The Four Agreements" by Don Miguel Ruiz - This book outlines four principles for living a fulfilling life, including the importance of being impeccable with your word, not taking things personally, and always doing your best.

SOURCES

(Not a complete list)

Credibility: How leaders gain and lose it, why people demand it (2nd ed.). San Francisco, CA: Jossey-Bass. Nehemiah, O. A. (2018).

Ryan, R. M., & Deci, E. L. (2017). Self-determination theory: Basic psychological needs in motivation, development, and wellness. New York, NY: Guilford Press.

Sinek, S. (2009). Start with why: How great leaders inspire everyone to take action. New York, NY: Penguin Group.

Stosny, S. (2007). A new psychology of love, traditional values and spiritual growth. New York, NY: Free Press.

The Dalai Lama. (2008). The universe in a single atom: The convergence of science and spirituality. New York, NY: Three Rivers Press.

www.ingramcontent.com/pod-product-compliance
Lightning Source LLC
Chambersburg PA
CBHW071025260726
48662CB00024B/2044